Faith in a Crisis

Faith in a Crisis

Famine, eviction and the church in North and South Uist

Flora Johnston

The Islands Book Trust

Published in 2012 by The Islands Book Trust

www.theislandsbooktrust.com

Copyright remains with the named author. Other than brief extracts for the purpose of review, no part of this publication may be reproduced in any form without the written consent of the publisher and copyright owner.

© The Islands Book Trust 2012

ISBN: 978-1-907443-32-9

Text © Flora Johnston
All photographs © Sandy Morrison

All rights reserved. No part of this publication may be reproduced, stored in a retrieval system, or transmitted in any other form or by any means, electronic, mechanical, photocopying, recording or otherwise without the prior written permission of the publishers. This book may not be lent, hired out, resold or otherwise disposed of by way of trade in any form of binding or cover other than that in which it is published, without the prior consent of the publishers.

The Islands Book Trust, Ravenspoint Centre, Kershader, South Lochs, Isle of Lewis, HS2 9QA. Tel: 01851 880737

Typeset by Erica Schwarz
Cover design by James Hutcheson
Printed and bound by Martins the Printers, Berwick upon Tweed

*For my father, Peter Keith Morrison, grandson of
Seoc of Rucaidh and Marion McVicar*

Contents

List of illustrations ix
Preface xi

Introduction 1
What happened in Uist? 3

The Men of God 7
Who were the ministers? 9
The short sermons of the ebb: Finlay Macrae and the Established Church 11
A modern Lochinvar: Finlay's powerful connections 13
My heart followed you closely: Norman Macleod and the Free Church 16
Schisms and divisions: the Disruption in North Uist 19
Widely and favourably known: the clergy of the south 23

Poverty and Famine 27
On the eve of starvation: famine comes to Uist 29
The chastening hand of our Heavenly Father: the Protestant response 33
A fortunate accident? Norman Macleod 37
The deepest melancholy: the clergy of the south 39

Eviction and Emigration 43

The rage for emigration: leaving the islands 45

Notice to remove: clearance 48

We will be left with the dregs: was denomination the cause? 52

Religion is not averse to the duty: Finlay Macrae and the Established Church 55

The Christian duty of non-resistance: Norman Macleod and the Free Church 59

They are much attached to the soil: John Chisholm and the clergy of the south 64

A Fresh Perspective 67

A different system of management: Thomas McLauchlan and a challenge to emigration 69

Conclusion 75

Notes 77

Bibliography 82

Illustrations

North Uist
1. Lochmaddy Pier
2. The ruins of Sponish House (now rebuilt), home of the Shaws
3. The 'Committee Road'
4. Kilmuir Church, once the parish church of North Uist
5. Finlay Macrae's now ruined farmhouse on Vallay, seen from across the strand
6. The Established Church and manse at Trumisgarry, where Norman Macleod ministered until the Disruption
7. The Free Church and manse at Paible, which were only built once Lord Macdonald had sold his estate
8. Balranald House, North Uist

South Uist
9. The grave of Father James MacGregor
10. Interior of the Roman Catholic church at Iochdar
11. Interior of the Roman Catholic church at Ardkenneth
12. Church of Scotland at Howmore
13. Interior of the church at Howmore, with its traditional central communion table
14. Roman Catholic church at Bornish
15. Interior of the church at Bornish

All photographs by Sandy Morrison

THE ISLANDS BOOK TRUST –
high quality books on island themes in English and Gaelic

Based in Lewis, the Islands Book Trust are a charity committed to furthering understanding and appreciation of the history of Scottish islands in their wider Celtic and Nordic context. We do this through publishing books, organising talks and conferences, visits, radio broadcasts, research and education on island themes. For details of membership of the Book Trust, which will keep you in touch with all our publications and other activities, see www.theislandsbooktrust.com or phone 01851 880737.

The Islands Book Trust, Ravenspoint, Kershader, South Lochs, Isle of Lewis, HS2 9QA (01851 880737)

Preface

This book explores the role of the clergy during a period of famine, emigration and eviction in North and South Uist. It offers an outline of the main events of the period but does not attempt to examine in detail the causes or implications of the 'Highland crisis', which have been explored elsewhere. Nor does it offer more than a cursory glimpse into the faith perspective of the ordinary people when faced with turmoil and hardship, although that too would make a fascinating study. Instead, *Faith in a Crisis* looks in detail at the role of the ministers and priests of these islands, focussing in particular on three individual clergymen. Using official reports submitted by the clergymen themselves, alongside other contemporary evidence such as letters and newspaper reports, it is possible to build up a picture of their actions and motivations during this time of appalling crisis.

Introduction

The mid-19th century was a turbulent period in the Highlands and Islands of Scotland. Broad themes of social and economic change, eviction and emigration, famine and poverty and religious controversy played out on a grand scale across the region.

Many of the judgements which have been made about the key players in the events of the time – the landlords, the factors, the clergy, and the people – have been made on that same grand scale.

But when we look at an individual community, the picture becomes more focussed, more intense, and more human. Many of the key features of a changing Highland society can be seen, with the distinctive colour of local context, in the islands of North Uist, Benbecula and South Uist.

This chain of islands, linked today by causeways, lies around 40 miles to the west of the mainland. It is a beautiful place, with long sandy beaches, windswept machair lands, dark silent pools and peaty moorland. The people of these islands were profoundly affected by the sweeping changes taking place in Highland society in the mid-19th century. The collapse of the kelp industry precipitated a crisis which would lead to mass emigration, and some of Scotland's most notorious examples of clearance. The failure of the potato crop, on which so many were dependent, brought parts of the population to the brink of starvation.

The church had a central role in society, but that role was made more complex by the Disruption of 1843, which saw the formation of the Free Church of Scotland. The religious dimension is particularly interesting in these interlinked islands,

Faith in a Crisis

where the Established Church, the Free Church and the Roman Catholic Church existed side by side.

The clergy, particularly those belonging to the Established Church, have often been attacked for their complicity with the landlords during these years of crisis across the Highlands.

So what was the situation in Uist when the people faced such hardship? Who were the ministers and priests of Uist during these troubled years? What did they say and do in response to the events unfolding around them?

Did they betray their people?

Introduction

What happened in Uist?

At the start of the 19th century the islands were in the hands of traditional proprietors, whose families had been chiefs and landowners in the Highlands for many generations. North Uist was owned by Lord Macdonald, who also had estates in Skye, and Benbecula and South Uist largely belonged to Clanranald. The factors who administered their estates were sometimes local men and sometimes incomers.

The economy of the islands had become heavily dependent on the kelp industry, in which seaweed was collected from the shores and burnt to create an ash which could be used in various chemical processes, including the manufacture of soap and glass. The work was labour intensive, and was so vital to the finances of the landlords that they imported workers and tried to prevent emigration. The people relied on the wages they received to pay their rent.

As early as the 1790s, the minister of North Uist, Allan MacQueen, recognised the importance of kelp to the survival of the islanders.

> The price has been on the decline, on account of the importation of great quantities of barilla and pot-ashes; and it is now so low that it is to be feared the manufacturing of it will be given up entirely (to the utter ruin of the tenants of this parish).[i]

By the 1820s the industry was in permanent decline, the landlords were facing economic meltdown and the people no longer had the money to pay their rents. In an attempt to make their estates profitable once more, the landlords turned to the creation of large sheep farms, let out to new tenants. The increasing population, which had been so important to the kelp industry, was now a costly drain on resources. Across North Uist, Benbecula and South Uist, people were cleared from some of the most profitable land.

Faith in a Crisis

Many were assisted to emigrate to Canada while others were moved onto poorer land which was already over-populated. The practice of subdividing crofts added to the population pressure. Duncan Shaw, factor for Clanranald, explained his frustration with current patterns of land use in a letter dated February 1827 to his employer's solicitor.

> You will not fail to observe the great numbers of subtenants on this Estate. This is a miserable system and it is particularly desirable that it should be got rid of. With a few exceptions, the Tacksmen are miserably poor; very bad farmers, following the old system of farming with very little improvement. They are very bad payers of rent and of course their Tenants cannot be in good circumstances. It is a great object for Clanranald to introduce Strangers instead of these Tacksmen, but this he can never do without getting rid of the Population.[ii]

It was an economy under immense pressure, and the failure of the potato crop in 1846 and in the years which followed brought it to disaster.

Periods of hunger and distress brought on by poor harvests were well-known in the experience of the islanders, but the events of the 1840s reached new depths. The economic changes of the past decades had led to an over-dependence on the potato as the main subsistence food for the people in the area. *A bliadhna ghais am buntata* or 'the year the potato wasted away', was followed in 1846–7 by a period of terrible destitution, which was exacerbated by a series of further bad harvests. Some assistance was provided by the government and by various charitable bodies, including the newly-created Free Church of Scotland, but the landlords were understood to have an obligation for the welfare of their people. Clanranald by this time had sold his estates to a wealthy Aberdeenshire man, Colonel John Gordon of Cluny. After a period of administration by trustees, Macdonald was forced

Introduction

to sell up in 1855. The financial pressures facing the landlords coupled with the destitution of the people gave a further impetus to the idea of persuading or forcing large numbers to emigrate. Evictions and assisted emigration continued over a long number of years, but between 1848 and 1852 examples of forced clearance from both North and South Uist caught the attention of the media, and became notorious scars upon the reputation of the islands, remembered to this day.

The 'clearances', and the events which surrounded them, soon became one of the most emotive and bitter issues of Highland history. Journalists of the time and later writers like John Prebble condemned the landlords who initiated them for callously betraying their submissive and helpless dependents. The factors who carried out the dirty work have equally had their names blackened by their deeds. But alongside the landlords and factors, the clergy too have been seen as culpable in the events of the mid-19th century. As recently as September 2000, in a debate on the Highland clearances in the Scottish Parliament, this statement was made:

> I suggest that our clergy and state church of the time were as guilty as anybody of encouraging the scourge of the clearances. Through their pious pronouncements from their pulpits they declared regularly that this was God's will for His devoted people, and as good and decent Christians they should accept His command and leave their shielings and holdings. But for the benefit of what? The great white sheep that were being introduced to the Highlands. They were considered to be more profitable than the indigenous population, and probably easier to manage and control. (John Munro, LD MSP for Ross, Skye and Inverness West)[iii]

A damning indictment of the men of the cloth.

The Men of God

Who were the ministers?

In North Uist, Benbecula and South Uist, three denominations existed side by side. North Uist was almost entirely Protestant, with two Established Church buildings at Kilmuir and at Trumisgarry, and a 'mission' at Carinish. The leading Established Church figure throughout the period was Finlay Macrae, who was minister of Kilmuir for forty years. The minister at Trumisgarry, Norman Macleod, joined the Free Church at the Disruption of 1843, along with the majority of the population of the island. He then remained as the only permanent Free Church minister for all three islands.

In South Uist the population was largely Roman Catholic, and was cared for throughout the period by two priests, John Chisholm and James MacGregor, along with a number of assistants. There was also an Established Church minister, Roderick Maclean, but his ill health and the small number of his parishioners meant that he played a very limited role. He was succeeded in 1854 by his son-in-law, Roderick Macdonald.

The people of Benbecula were divided between the different denominations, and they were largely cared for by temporary catechists and missionaries or the clergy of the islands to north and south.

The clergymen of these islands were, on the whole, not outsiders. They were highlanders themselves, born into the families of ministers or 'gentlemen farmers', Gaelic-speakers, and familiar with the culture, heritage, and lifestyles of their congregation. As individuals living in small communities, the networks of relationships which bound them to their parishioners are significant. To really understand what was going on at the time, we need to look closely at the individual clergymen, and to establish what we can about their backgrounds, their home and family circumstances, and the different elements of their lives which could affect their responses to this unfolding catastrophe.

The short sermons of the ebb:
Finlay Macrae and the Established Church

The parish church of North Uist was at Kilmuir, on the western side of the island, and its minister for forty years was the Rev. Finlay Macrae. Finlay played an active role throughout his long ministry in the events which unfolded in the island, a role which at the time and since has brought him both criticism and praise.

Finlay, from Lochcarron in the West Highlands, came to North Uist in 1815 as missionary to the Sand and Sollas district. In 1818, aged 26, he was ordained to the parish church at Kilmuir. The appointment rested with the patron, Lord Macdonald. Finlay remained as parish minister until his death in 1858.

Six years after becoming parish minister, Finlay married 24-year-old Isabella Maria Macdonald, the youngest daughter of Colonel Alexander Macdonald of Lynedale and Balranald. The Macdonalds of Balranald were one of the most influential families on the island. Isabella's oldest brother James was factor to Lord Macdonald, while another of her brothers, John, lived at Rodel House on Harris and was factor to the Harris landowner, the Earl of Dunmore. Both minister and factor were directly dependent on the goodwill and patronage of the landlord, and so the marriage of Finlay and Isabella confirmed and strengthened the social hierarchies of the day.

Finlay and Isabella made their home on the tidal island of Vallay, although the previous minister, William Arbuckle, had lived considerably nearer his church and people at Baleloch. In 1815 William Arbuckle had become minister of Kilmuir Church, built by his stonemason father John. John Arbuckle also built the house at Baleloch in 1816–17, but William died unexpectedly the following year. A valuable source for the study of North and South Uist is an unpublished history written by Church of Scotland minister Angus Macdonald in 1933, and it is Macdonald who tells us that Finlay 'was not content to live in the modest house at Baleloch'.[iv]

On Vallay Finlay, Isabella and their children occupied a substantial stone house built by James Gillespie Graham in the late 1790s. Sources agree that Finlay became very much a farmer first and minister second. The very distance, not to mention the inconvenience of dependence on tides, must surely have interfered with the minister's pastoral duties, while his sermons became known as '*sermon beag na traghad*' or the 'short sermons of the ebb' – cut short to allow Finlay to return home before the incoming tide![v] He and his brother-in-law James Macdonald of Balranald often vied to take the top prize for livestock at the agricultural fair. When he died in 1858, Finlay held the leases for the farms of Vallay and Griminish on North Uist, and Luskentyre on Harris, and his substantial estate was valued at more than £3800.[vi]

Finlay was very much at home in the Hebridean world, having grown up in Gaelic-speaking Lochcarron. His entry in the *New Statistical Account* reveals his love for Gaelic culture, describing the North Uist bard John MacCodrum as 'a poetical genius of the highest order' and the Gaelic tongue as 'a beautiful and expressive language.' He also had a great concern to extend the provision of education throughout the island.[vii]

Finlay died in 1858, and was succeeded by his son John Alexander. Perhaps it was hard to follow his forty year career – at any rate, John Alexander seemed never quite to live up to his father's reputation as a farmer or a minister. Angus Macdonald described him as 'a most amiable and kindly man, but not intellectual.'[viii] John himself somewhat ruefully stated to the Napier Commission in 1884, 'I hold a glebe, and I used to farm it, but it turned out that I was a very bad farmer, and I let it out to a tenant.'[ix] Nor was his ministry entirely successful, and in 1886, with an alleged drink problem and a declining congregation, he was persuaded to resign.

A modern Lochinvar:
Finlay's powerful connections

Perhaps no incident highlights the close relationships between various establishment figures in North Uist better than the dramatic love story of 1850 which was reported in newspapers nationwide as 'A Modern Lochinvar'.

Jessie Macdonald was the twenty-one-year-old daughter of James Thomas Macdonald of Balranald – also known as Seumas Ruadh – and thus was a niece of Isabella and Finlay. Jessie was in love with Donald Macdonald of Monkstadt, Skye, who for a few months in 1849 served as factor in North Uist, living at Baleloch.

1849 was a turbulent year in North Uist. As factor, Donald was involved in the attempted clearance of the Sollas district. The *Inverness Advertiser* for 14 August 1849 records, 'The sheriffs were accompanied by Mr Cooper, and they were here joined by Mr Macdonald, the young factor for Lord Macdonald.'

Patrick Cooper, an Aberdeenshire man, was trustee for the heavily indebted Macdonald estates and the main instigator of the Sollas evictions. But Cooper and Donald Macdonald would soon both take part in another, far more personal drama.

While Cooper was in North Uist he would undoubtedly have visited Balranald House, and he too was attracted to young Jessie. Jessie's attachment to Donald Macdonald stood in the way, and Donald was conveniently dismissed from his post in October. In the subsequent trial relating to the events which followed, Cooper claimed that Donald had never really been factor, and that he himself had taken over collecting the rents on Lord Macdonald's request purely for reasons of convenience.

In February 1850 Cooper proposed to Jessie, and it is clear that her father was in favour of the match. In desperation, Jessie wrote to Donald, and the young couple planned to elope together. On the arranged night, Jessie escaped from Balranald House, and she and Donald made for Lochmaddy. Donald's servant, who helped them, said, 'The lady was very anxious to be off, and they went as fast as their horses could carry them,' – and he added that Jessie was laughing.

From Lochmaddy the plan was to sail to Skye, but it was a stormy night. They ended up at Harris. By this time the alarm had been raised, and they were soon discovered by John, brother of Seumas Ruadh (and of Isabella) and factor to the Earl of Dunmore. Jessie was taken to her uncle's home, Rodel House, and held there. His wife slept in the bedroom with her to prevent her escaping, and a police guard was put in place to watch the house.

Donald gathered some friends from Skye, and they sailed to Harris to rescue Jessie by night. Newspaper accounts state that 'Mr Macdonald (Rodil) came out of the house in his shirt and drawers, swearing at them as if he was mad.' Somehow, in the ensuing confusion, Jessie and Donald managed to make their escape. They headed for the mainland, and were later married in Edinburgh. The two brothers, Seumas Ruadh and John of Rodel, together with Patrick Cooper, were not likely to accept such defiance easily. Donald Macdonald and two of his accomplices were charged with breaking into Rodel House and assaulting the inhabitants, in a trial which excited widespread interest, but they were found not guilty – to cheers from the public gallery. Donald and Jessie later emigrated to Australia.[x]

These events took place in the very close circle of family and friends of Finlay and Isabella. The register of marriages for Kilmuir parish, North Uist, has the following intriguing entry, surely authorised by Finlay:

> Donald MacDonald Tacksman of Baleloch to Jessie Cathrine MacDonald daughter of James Thomas MacDonald Esquire Tacksman of Balranald 31st March 1850.[xi]

The Men of God

In actual fact, Jessie and Donald were married on 22 April in St Cuthbert's parish, Edinburgh. The entry describes them both as living at 20 Gilmore Place in that parish.[xii] A Church of Scotland marriage required banns to be proclaimed in the home parish of both bride and groom on three separate occasions, usually three Sundays, before the wedding. Does the North Uist entry suggest that Jessie and Donald's banns were proclaimed in Kilmuir Church? Imagine the atmosphere! Or was the entry some attempt to give respectability to the whole affair?

The very next entry in the Kilmuir register records the marriage of another Balranald daughter, Elizabeth, to a Skye minister, also in April 1850. The entry records that the banns were, 'proclaimed in the Parish Church in North Uist in the regular and normal manner' – a statement that is not made with regard to Jessie's marriage. No doubt Finlay, his brother-in-law Seumas Ruadh, and everyone else concerned, took far more pleasure in Elizabeth's wedding!

On the night of the census of March 1851, just over a year after these dramatic events, Isabella, her eldest son and her daughter-in-law were staying with her brother John at Rodel House, scene of Jessie's imprisonment. Minister, factor, land agent … they were bound together very closely indeed.

My heart followed you closely:
Norman Macleod and the Free Church

In the early 19th century 32 new churches, known as 'parliamentary churches', were built across the Highlands to a design by Thomas Telford, to meet the needs of people in scattered parishes. They included Trumisgarry Church, built in 1828 to serve the northern district of Sand and Sollas. In 1835, Norman Macleod came to be its minister.

Norman came from a well-known Skye family. Immediately before coming to North Uist he served as a missionary in Saltcoats, and a Gaelic poem laments his departure to Uist:

Fhuair mi milis do chàinnt
'S lean mo chridhe riut teann,
'S cha robh coimeas riut leam 'san sgireachd

I found your speech sweet
And my heart followed you closely,
And there was not your equal, to my mind, in the parish.[xiii]

Norman was 34 years old when he came to North Uist. His sister Anne already lived on the island, married to Duncan Shaw, who at various times had served as factor on the estates of South Uist, North Uist and Harris. The Shaws lived at Sponish House in Lochmaddy, an imposing mansion built for the then factor in 1801. Their son Charles would become Sheriff, and was involved in dealing with the issues of famine and clearance.

Three years after taking up his post Norman, like Finlay, married a young woman from North Uist and became part of an intricate network of family relationships. Norman's wife Julia was the daughter of Dr Alexander Macleod, or '*An Dotair Ban*', and granddaughter of Dr Murdoch Macleod of Kilpheder, two well-known Uist figures.

Murdoch and his wife Mary Maclean had been part of an earlier emigration from Uist, settling for a while in North Carolina in the 1770s. They returned to Uist after being caught up in the American Revolution. Their eldest daughter Flora married Rev. William Arbuckle, predecessor of Finlay Macrae. *An Dotair Ban* was celebrated for his medical skills but also worked as factor on the South Uist estates. His legacy is hard to judge. On the one hand he appears to have been held in high regard as a doctor but his reputation was tainted by association with the clearances carried out by John Gordon of Cluny, and he was criticised by some of those who gave evidence to the Napier Commission.

An Dotair Ban's older daughter Julia married Norman, and his second daughter Jane married John McIver, minister of Harris.

So Norman, like Finlay, was connected to various influential people on the island, whose actions during the crises of famine and eviction would impact so profoundly on the lives of the people. Duncan Shaw was his brother-in-law and Charles Shaw was his nephew, while through his wife he was related to the Macleod and Arbuckle families.

Norman himself was a man of strong principle, and from the outset was at odds on many church issues with his neighbour, Finlay Macrae. In 1843, when divisions in the church culminated in the Disruption, Norman left the Church of Scotland. *The Annals of the Free Church of Scotland* record:

> Norman Macleod, minister of Trumisgarry Parliamentary Church, in the parish of North Uist, 'came out' in 1843, and for some years had charge of almost the whole of the long island, the remainder being served by a catechist.

The charge was not sanctioned until 1849, and Mr Macleod did not manage to obtain a manse and church until 1858.[xiv] These years, which coincided with the worst period of poverty and evictions, were years of instability and uncertainty for the Free Church on Uist, and also for Norman and his young family. He would however spend the rest of his life, until his death aged 80 in 1881, as Free Church minister on North Uist.

Schisms and divisions:
the Disruption in North Uist

When Norman Macleod came to North Uist in 1835, he arrived in a religious environment which was rife with faction and separation. Norman himself described this to the Select Committee on Sites for Churches in 1847. Describing a house used for worship within his parish, he said 'It was occupied by the people themselves before I was settled in the place; they were not satisfied with their minister, and they began to meet for worship in this place.' He claimed that they held their own services and did not go to the Established Church, even for baptisms.[xv]

One historian of North Uist, Ewen MacRury, himself a Free Church minister, tells that in the early 19th century a lay evangelist came to the island and 'a religious revival followed which completely altered the outlook of many people who had been indifferent to the Gospel.'[xvi] The concerns of the Established Church over this were repeatedly expressed in Presbytery minutes. In 1829 they pleaded for a minister for the mission of Sand and Sollas, because 'fanaticism and sectarianism are making rapid progress in this extensive parish.'[xvii] Similarly in 1841, Finlay stated that 'There is at present in the parish a catechist employed by the Highland Missionary Society. He officiates as a lay preacher; but does not consider himself subject to the control of, and is not acknowledged by, the Established Church'.[xviii]

Couched within the formal, legal language of the Presbytery minutes, the mounting tension among the ministers is evident. Finlay and Norman stood firmly on either side of the division which was deepening within the Established Church. Norman was repeatedly the sole dissenter from decisions taken at presbytery, and as early as 1839 Finlay Macrae accused him of admitting a separatist to communion in his church and 'thus encouraging schisms and divisions, against the law and practice of the church.'[xix] In 1840, Finlay and Norman came into conflict over a sermon preached by Finlay at the opening of the Synod of Glenelg. This related to the controversial Veto Act, which gave congregations the right to reject a minister nominated by their patron. Norman was among those who objected to Finlay's sermon, leading to an investigation by the General Assembly. Finlay was later cleared of any charge of unsound doctrine, but it can't have done much to improve relations between the two men.

In 1843, Norman Macleod was one of those who finally left the Established Church, forming the new Free Church of Scotland in the event known as the Disruption. The central issue was the right of the people to choose their own minister. In North Uist the effect of the Disruption was momentous. The large majority of the people followed Norman into the Free Church, and the atmosphere of hostility and suspicion became more apparent at all levels of society.

In his unpublished history of North Uist, Angus Macdonald speaks of the time with his customary dislike for the seceders, but in doing so he vividly conveys the relationship between the two churches.

> If ever the Devil was raised in North Uist it was in 1843. Men cut each other dead on the high road. If by any chance two men spoke it was to vilify one another. The Free Church man was always the aggressor; the other was a black Moderate on the defensive, who, when he struck out, gave as much as he got and perhaps a little more … Fanatics were let loose, and the old Church was denounced as nothing better than a Synagogue of Satan. Its ministers were stipend lifters and worse. They and their adherents were loaded with the most opprobrious epithets. They were beyond the pale of salvation. It was an awful time.[xx]

The Men of God

Closely intertwined with the division was the relationship with the landlords. Finlay Macrae, as an Established Church minister, was dependent on his landlord for stipend, glebe and house. The Disruption was in part a rejection of the power of the landlords over the people. Norman, by quitting his church at Trumisgarry, was no longer entitled to his house. He wrote to Lord Macdonald, offering to pay the same rent as any other and observing, 'I trust your Lordship does not really intend to drive me with my young and helpless family out of my present dwelling house.' The factor, Seumas Ruadh of Balranald, himself an Established Church elder, replied in these terms:

> It is not [his Lordship's] intention either to grant you a site or to give you any lands. ... I am sorry for you and your family, you will be much put about, but you have brought it all on yourself. ... Kind compliments to Mrs McLeod.

At this time Norman was offered the chance to return to Saltcoats, but stayed where the Free Church believed he was of greatest use.[xxi] The Macleod family spent over a decade moving between different houses on the island, sometimes staying with friends and relatives. In the 1851 census they can be found living with some of Julia's Arbuckle relatives. The people who had chosen to join the Free Church similarly feared that the landlord would hold this against them when considering their leases. This became a particularly contentious issue as families were cleared from the land.

Lord Macdonald also refused to allow the new Free Church on North Uist a site for a place of worship. An attempt to build an unauthorised meeting place at Paible was prevented by Balranald, who got together the carts of those tenants who had remained with the Established Church and used them to carry away the building stones. For long years the people met in the open air for worship when the weather allowed, and in their own small houses

21

Faith in a Crisis

at other times. Norman described the difficulty of conducting worship in these circumstances:

> Sometimes they are obliged to have a horse or a cow in one end of the house, and we assemble at the other end. We are often interrupted by hens, and the squalling of children, and smoke. I was often very hoarse after coming out, owing to the action of the smoke on my throat and lungs.[xxii]

The hostility between the two denominations allegedly extended to the pulpit, at least on behalf of Finlay. He remained a convinced supporter of the Established Church despite the defection of his own brother, also a minister, to the Free Church. Norman's evidence to the Committee continued:

> I was told that [Finlay Macrae] is in the habit of alluding to the Free Church in terms of condemnation or disapprobation in the pulpit ... I seldom or never allude to the Establishment in my discourses. I do not think I have done so half a dozen times since the disruption; nor did I ever at all call upon a person to leave the Establishment and join the Free Church, either in public or private.[xxiii]

Established Church Presbytery minutes from soon after the Disruption, however, complained that Macleod and others 'of the very wildest description' were making great effort 'to persuade and even frighten the people to leave the Established Church'.[xxiv]

By the time of the Disruption land reorganisation was already underway, and the years of greatest famine were just around the corner. Meanwhile, the divisions and suspicions which had already existed before 1843 were now clear for all to see. It is not surprising that, as we shall see, many believed that religious denomination was a significant factor in the events which unfolded over the next few years.

Widely and favourably known: the clergy of the south

The population of South Uist, like the islands of Eriskay and Barra which lay further south again, was largely Roman Catholic. Throughout the period, two priests cared for the people of South Uist, with help from various assistants. There was also a priest on Barra. James MacGregor was based in the north of South Uist at Iochdar, and John Chisholm was further south at Bornish.

James MacGregor was born in Perthshire, and came to South Uist in 1828. According to Angus Macdonald's manuscript history, he was 'widely and favourably known in the Long Island', and was particularly famed for his medical knowledge. His neighbour in the south, John Chisholm, had been in South Uist since 1819. Both men remained as priests throughout the period, and they died in the same year. MacGregor had met with an accident in 1865 which left him unable to continue his duties, and he died in February 1867 aged 78. John Chisholm died 5 months later, in July, at the age of 72.

Both priests are remembered for their efforts to provide adequate meeting places for their members. James MacGregor went to Ireland in 1836 to collect money for the erection of the *Eaglais Mhor an Iochdair*, or 'the big church at Iochdar', and Chisholm was responsible for building chapels at Daliburgh and Bornish during this period. The priests, like the ministers of the Protestant churches, also farmed the land on which they lived.[xxv]

A series of letters between John Chisholm and his bishop, Andrew Scott, sheds light on the life and ministry of the South Uist priests. Bishop Scott encouraged the priests to keep on good terms with the landlords, and saw the arrival of a new landowner, Gordon of Cluny, as an opportunity.

> Were the Catholics to submit implicitly and apparently with cheerfulness to all his plans and to all his orders whatever they may be, and to speak always favourably of him, and if the protestants were to thwart him in anything, the whole island would soon become entirely Catholic. For some years it will require very great prudence on the part of the Catholic Clergymen and on the part of the poor Catholics, and if you will always act according to what I have said, you will find it will ultimately be for your own interest and for the interest of Religion in these Islands.[xxvi]

Despite this advice, the bishop's letters reveal that James MacGregor, priest at Iochdar, was for a time at odds with Cluny over the sale of some cattle, and in his book *The Catholic Highlands of Scotland,* Odo Blundell states that John Chisholm was 'a giant who could have thrown the factor – with whom he often had a disagreement – over the wall'.[xxvii] Nevertheless, the priests entered the period of crisis being urged to appease their landlord for the greater benefit of the Catholic faith. How would that affect their response to the events which unfolded?

There was also one Established Church minister based on South Uist, and one on Barra, again assisted at times by catechists and missionaries. A native of Skye, Roderick Maclean served firstly as assistant in South Uist and then succeeded as minister to the small Protestant population of the island in 1833. By this time he was already over 60 years old. There was no church and no manse. His health was not good, and his ministry appears to have been particularly ineffective. He rarely attended Presbytery meetings. In 1848, concern about the condition of the Established Church at South Uist was expressed at the General Assembly:

> In South Uist ... the sacrament had not been administered for seven years, and had only been administered three times during the whole incumbency of the present minister, and the parish

The Men of God

had continued without a place of worship since the time of the Reformation ... If he was old and had long neglected his parish, the system was to blame which did not provide a retiring allowance for him.[xxviii]

Roderick Maclean died in 1854, and was succeeded by his son-in-law Roderick Macdonald, who came from North Uist. *Fasti Ecclesiae Scoticanae*, the record of ministers of the Church of Scotland, described him as 'A man of high attainments and of varied culture, he excelled as a preacher in Gaelic and in English.' Roderick was still minister at the time of the Napier Commission in 1883, and was described as 'a good friend to the country' in the evidence of one Roman Catholic witness. However, in his manuscript history of the islands, Angus Macdonald was less enthusiastic about the younger Roderick, describing him as:

> A gifted man and one of the best preachers in the Highlands. But what of it all? He rested on his oars at once, took to farming, the curse of all his predecessors, and went to seed.[xxix]

In Barra the minister from May 1847 was Henry Beatson, a Greenock man whose name has been unfavourably linked with Cluny's policies of eviction.

Relations between the denominations in South Uist were far friendlier than in North Uist. Although Free Church and Established Church shared much common ground theologically, the recent separation had caused real hurt and bitterness. By contrast in South Uist, at least on a daily and superficial level, Catholics and Protestants had long since learned to co-exist at peace and to work together for the good of the people.

Despite this the Roman Catholic priests remained wary of anything which might suggest an attempt to weaken the Catholic faith of the people. They were anxious that Catholic children would not be required to learn any part of the Protestant catechism in school. James MacGregor's concern to protect the faith of his flock is revealed in one letter he wrote to a priest in Glasgow about a South Uist boy, Malcolm Martin. The son of a Catholic mother and Protestant father, Malcolm had been sent by the South Uist factor to work on the Clyde 'perhaps with the view that he would there learn a trade and forget the Roman Catholic religion at the same time'. In explaining Malcolm's position and urging his fellow priest to look after the boy, James MacGregor stated that his widowed mother:

> had not the hardihood to bring up her children in her own faith for fear of drawing down upon herself and upon her destitute progeny the resentment of their protestant relations and of the Factor's family, which is all powerful in the Country and happens to be besotted admirers of the gospel ideas of John Knox.[xxx]

The only evidence of open dispute between minister and priest on South Uist regards the erection of a bell on the chapel at Bornish. Roderick Maclean wished to have this removed and consulted the Presbytery for advice. On being approached on the matter, John Chisholm wrote to Bishop Scott to discover what his own position was. The Presbytery stated that 'the Law of the Land justified Mr Maclean to get this cause of offence removed', whilst Bishop Scott wrote to John Chisholm that 'there is no civil law of the land preventing you from putting up a Bell on your Chapel.'[xxxi] No record is made of the immediate outcome of the dispute.

Poverty and Famine

On the eve of starvation: famine comes to Uist

The people of Uist were already accustomed to difficult years. Presbytery minutes frequently recorded the inability of the congregations to contribute to church collections. Similarly in May 1832, John Chisholm wrote to Bishop Scott, 'I never saw the island scarcer of money than it is at present. It is a rare thing to see a shilling among the people. I trust however matters will soon change to the better.'[xxxii] In 1837, he told the *Commission for Religious Instruction* that he couldn't visit distant parts of his parish because 'the people are so extremely poor that he cannot obtain accommodation among them for a night.'[xxxiii]

In 1842 Roderick Maclean responded to a request for money from officials in Govan seeking to reclaim expenses relating to the death of a South Uist man, in these terms:

> There are no funds whatsoever in this parish for such purpose, or any purpose whatever of the kind, the people being so poor, and unable to make Sabbath church collections; the poor or paupers being solely supported by the tenantry, three-fourths of whom are Catholics.[xxxiv]

In 1843–4 the Poor Law Inquiry gathered evidence from parishes across the country. Donald Macdonald, priest on Barra, described the growing destitution of his people and observed that 'Potatoes and barley bread, when they can procure it, are the common food of the greater number of people in this district. Very often nothing but potatoes and salt.'[xxxv]

By this time, the combined factors of the failure of the kelp industry, the creation of enlarged sheep farms and the subdivision of crofts meant that many families were trying to make a living from a very small piece of land. This encouraged dependence on the potato, a crop which could be successfully raised in such circumstances. But within two years of Donald Macdonald giving his evidence to the Poor Law Inquiry, that crop had failed and the people were starving.

The potato disease struck first in Ireland, where the consequences were utterly devastating. Across Scotland, the proportion of the population affected was far smaller and the relief effort far more effective than in Ireland. Nevertheless, the failure of the potato crop ushered in years of suffering and misery for the people of North and South Uist.

The situation was at its most severe on South Uist and Barra, the estates which largely belonged to the rich new landowner from Aberdeenshire, John Gordon of Cluny. By autumn 1846 it was clear that a grave crisis was unfolding. In November 1846 the minute of the parish board of South Uist, signed by Roderick Maclean, read:

> The Board exceedingly regret that it is their principal duty to state the deplorable condition of hundreds of families throughout the parish, who entirely depended upon the potato crop, which has completely failed, and have now no resource whatever to support themselves and families; so that, unless some immediate relief is afforded, the consequences must be that they shall starve; and even those in better circumstances will have no seed to put in the ground next season.[xxxvi]

Sheriff Charles Shaw of Lochmaddy, nephew of Norman Macleod of the Free Church, played a significant part in drawing the attention of the government authorities to the desperate condition of the people. He wrote a letter which was passed to the Lord Advocate, and which laid out the situation in stark terms.

Poverty and Famine

> A large portion of the people of this district are on the eve of starvation. They subsist on, perhaps, a little fish or shell-fish, without either vegetables, gruel or anything else, and of this half a meal a-day is all that in many cases can be procured. I am told that two have died in Barra of starvation, one of them a young man under 20, and the other a woman considerably advanced in life. Even in this parish, in which want of food is not yet so general, there are many cases of extreme destitution.

Charles went on to ask for advice. Should he make judicial enquiry into the reported deaths by starvation? He had heard that the people were afraid to seek poor relief for fear of the displeasure of the proprietor. He went on 'I feel a responsibility hanging over me when I know the state of the people, and that their only legal chance of relief, which is through myself, is shut up by distance and other obstacles.'

On receiving this letter, the Lord Advocate stated that 'It grieves me to the heart to think that destitution should have made a progress so stern and alarming on a property belonging to one of the most wealthy proprietors in this country.' The direct result of Charles Shaw's letter was that the authorities sent Captain Pole to investigate the state of affairs on Cluny's lands, and also supplied grain to be sold 'at a fair price'. They entered into correspondence with Cluny himself, pointing out his duty and the options available to him. The crisis gained national attention. Cluny was criticised for failing to help his people, and for bringing to a stop the improvement works which enabled them to earn money just at the time when they were most needed. Cluny was defensive, and simply denied that help was needed. He criticised the supply of additional grain, saying 'I shall be greatly surprised if Captain Pole does not find the people supplied with food before he arrives, in which case I shall feel it a very great grievance to be compelled to pay so highly for what cannot be wanted, at least for a time, and must daily be getting injured by vermin and a lack of convenience for stowing it away.'[xxxvii]

In North Uist, while the crisis did not reach quite the same levels as further south, the failure of the potato crop similarly caused great hardship. Angus Macdonald described the scene in 1847 at the home of Charles Shaw in Lochmaddy:

> [His] house at Sponish was surrounded by crowds of people asking for meal or provisions of any kind, some of them in tears imploring for sustenance for their famishing families.[xxxviii]

The chastening hand of our Heavenly Father: the Protestant response

So how did the churches respond to this crisis, both locally and nationally?

Both Protestant denominations understood the problems facing the Highlands to be a sign of God's displeasure with his people. Thus, at the General Assembly of the Church of Scotland in 1847, the statement was made that:

> The General Assembly, having taken into their serious consideration the Overture anent the prevailing Famine and Distress in many parts of Ireland and the Highlands of Scotland, most earnestly call upon all the Members of this Church to humble themselves before God, and to regard this National Calamity as a requirement from Him to confess their sins, and amend their ways and doings.[xxxix]

The Free Church similarly called for 'a day of humiliation and prayer'.[xl] Yet although both churches believed that the famine was sent from God as a call to the people to return, they did not use this belief to avoid responsibility for practical assistance. On the contrary, the idea of famine as judgement of God was used to promote practical help in the Highlands, and the call for prayer was clearly linked with a call for money.

> The General Assembly further enjoin us all the Ministers of this Church to avail themselves of every proper opportunity … for directing the attention of the people to the recent dispensations of Providence, and for inculcating the duty of continuing to express by their prayers, and also, where they have it in their power, by their alms, their heartfelt sympathy with the thousands of their fellow-subjects who are suffering the severities of famine.[xli]

Faith in a Crisis

TM Devine has explored in detail the outstanding response of the Free Church of Scotland to the crisis.[xlii] Their efforts were crucial in the provision of relief, particularly during the months after the famine first struck. The Free Church had a huge following in destitute areas, but also had strong support in the cities where people were both anxious and able to assist their fellow seceders in the north-west. The aid provided by the Free Church was not however distributed along denominational lines. In South Uist, where the Free Church following was minimal and most people were Roman Catholics, Charles Shaw commented 'At present our only hopes are placed on the Free Church, whose conduct has been truly noble.'[xliii]

Norman Macleod, Free Church minister in Uist, was heavily involved in distributing aid among the people. When appealing to Lord Macdonald to be allowed to remain in his house, he referred to his efforts to assist the people and also revealed his own belief that the famine was a rebuke from God.

> Will your Lordship allow me to observe, without offence, that at a time when we are all suffering under the chastening hand of our Heavenly Father, it looks somewhat unseemly that we should be the occasion of suffering to one another. I have already taken the principal part in distributing food, supplied by the Free Church, among your Lordship's cotters and crofters in this country. I am at this moment in the receipt of nearly £40 (I may say now £100) from respectable private parties in London, Edinburgh and Glasgow, with which I am helping to relieve much of the present distress, besides lessening the burden of supporting many of the people to your Lordship and tenants.[xliv]

Norman's counterpart Finlay Macrae, minister of the Established Church, was also involved in the relief effort in Uist. He welcomed to the island a leading Established Church minister, Dr Norman Macleod, was who a key figure in the attempts of the Established

Poverty and Famine

Church to bring relief to victims of the famine. Dr Macleod's own Established Church congregation in Glasgow was largely made up of Highlanders and those of Highland descent, and he worked tirelessly to raise and distribute funds for the benefit of the people. He worked closely with the Free Church, declaring:

> Dissenting clergymen are just as deserving of esteem as the Established clergy can be. They are a most respectable body, the dissenting clergy of Glasgow, just now; and I should think it invidious with regard to a fund which is collected from all, that the distribution should be given to one class of churches.[xlv]

Dr Macleod visited Uist in 1847. Angus Macdonald's unpublished history gives an account of the visit, and of Finlay's role at this time. Macdonald tells us that, on his arrival on North Uist, Dr Macleod went firstly to Vallay accompanied by Sheriff Shaw to meet with Finlay Macrae, and the three then proceeded to consult with the factor. On the Sunday, Dr Macleod preached in Macrae's church and, according to Macdonald, made a great impression on the people. Finlay Macrae is praised in this account, although once again his preference for the practical rather than the spiritual is noted.

> The Reverend Finlay Macrae rose to the occasion and played a prominent part, glad of the opportunity of standing anywhere except in the pulpit. Purely secular duties delighted his soul. This was a great play. He accompanied Dr Macleod to South Uist and afterwards went with him to Harris and so he earned the reputation of being a *deagh fhear duthcha* [good man to the country].[xlvi]

It seems Finlay the farmer had more than short term assistance in mind. In 1851 he entered into correspondence, published in the *Glasgow Herald*, about the possibility of cultivating flax on North Uist, to provide employment and lift the people out of poverty. With his interest in agriculture, Finlay was trying this out for himself:

> In order to try the success of the growth of flax in North Uist, and with a view of bettering, if possible, the suffering inhabitants, and of directing their attention to the culture of an article which may afford them remunerative employment; I have this season sown nearly two acres of ground with flax seed…'[xlvii]

Did Finlay and his Established Church colleagues on the islands really believe that the famine was a rebuke from God, as Norman Macleod of the Free Church clearly did? Quite possibly they did, but it is interesting to note that no direct reference to the social problems as the judgement and vengeance of God appears in the Uist Presbytery minutes of this period. In 1837, 1839, 1848 and 1853, Days of Thanksgiving for better harvests were proposed by the Presbytery. The entry for 1848 reads as follows:

> The Presbytery having taken into their consideration the blessing and favour of God in giving propitious weather for securing the crops of last harvest in good condition which must greatly alleviate the miseries of destitution still existing by the continued failure of the potato crop; and also considering that the bounds of this Presbytery are still free from the scourge of the cholera which has already appeared in other parts of the country, have resolved to appoint a day of thanksgiving to Almighty God in order to direct the minds of the people to both these objects.[xlviii]

Yet despite these repeated calls for Days of Thanksgiving for the provision of crops, no record exists of Uist Presbytery having carried out the instructions of the General Assembly to hold a Day of Humiliation to appease God. It is unlikely to have been omitted from the minutes, as the days of thanksgiving appear so regularly, so we may conclude that the local Presbytery did not carry out the national instruction on this occasion. Perhaps, surrounded by people who were poverty-stricken and starving, it was simply unthinkable.

A fortunate accident? Norman Macleod

Those on North Uist who were most vulnerable to the failure of the potato crop, and who were trying to scrape out a living from minimal resources, tended to belong to the Free Church. We have already seen that their minister, Norman Macleod, was concerned for their welfare and played a prominent role in distributing the aid supplied by the wider Free Church. But Norman's primary concern was always not just for the physical but also the spiritual condition of his people, as he sought to guide them in the godly way of living amidst their trials.

In the desperate winter of 1846–7 an event took place off the northern shores of North Uist which was seen by some as 'a fortunate accident.' A ship was lost between North Uist and Harris, and hundreds of barrels of flour were washed ashore. One government official involved in the relief effort described the shipwreck in these terms:

> The loss of a vessel upon North Uist, with £15,000 worth of flour and other provision, may prove a fortunate accident for the poor islanders.[xlix]

The *Inverness Courier* went further, describing the unexpected bounty as 'a strange intervention of Providence ... But for this opportune wreck deaths from starvation would have been numerous, as the natives had nothing to live upon but a little fish, without either meal or potatoes.'[l]

Norman Macleod, however, heard both of the shipwreck and of a plan by some of his flock to seize some of the flour. He quite clearly did not regard the provision of the flour as a gift from God but as a temptation to his suffering people to sin. He was fully aware of the difficulties they faced, but that did not justify unlawful behaviour. He intervened to prevent the theft of the flour.

> The people were beginning to get scarce, and to eat their seed corn; they were in that state that they were prepared to do anything desperate, in order to get food to save their seed. ... When this report reached me it was late in the week; I sent a confidential person to the people to dissuade them from it, with a strong remonstrance, showing the impropriety of it in every point of view. The people were gathered at the time the person arrived, with the intention of pledging themselves to proceed to business the next day; but such was the effect of my message to them that they separated very soon, and they did not proceed to take away the flour; and when I met some of them the next day, or a few days afterwards, and asked them why they had not taken the flour away, their answer was, 'How could we take it away after getting such a message from yourself?'[li]

Some of those who did steal the flour were in fact arrested, although the *Inverness Courier* urged leniency. It seems that both journalists and government ministers had some sympathy with the actions of starving people, but Norman Macleod viewed the world from an eternal perspective, and the spiritual salvation of his people was his first priority.

The deepest melancholy: the clergy of the south

In South Uist and Barra the situation by now was utterly desperate. Captain Pole's investigation and mercy mission of January 1847, prompted in part by the urgent letter of Charles Shaw, led him to meet with ministers, priests, factors and 'gentlemen farmers'. The Established Church had little impact. There was no Established Church minister on Barra, Alexander Nicolson having died in April 1846, and when Captain Pole visited his widow in the manse he heard a tale of starving people coming daily to the door to beg for food. Roderick Maclean, the frail minister of South Uist, does not feature in Captain Pole's report. Instead Pole met with priest John Chisholm and heard from him something of the extent of the misery:

> I found this gentleman impressed with the deepest melancholy on account of the state of the poor. He stated that it was indescribable; he knew no case of death from starvation; but it is inconceivable to what a pitch the poor are driven, and the quantity of food necessary for their support until next crops will be enormous. The people are constantly applying to him. Sickness is not prevalent, but he knows three cases in which he considers death was produced by the use of bad or deficient food. ... Every week for the last two months they have been expecting a supply of food from Colonel Gordon, but have been disappointed. The very poor must live as they can, and die as they can, unless speedily relieved. ... The Rev. Mr Chisholm concluded his tale of distress by adding that he had lately attended by the death-bed of a parishioner, whose only nourishment was an uncooked turnip by the bedside.

Pole also met with Cluny's factor, Dr Alexander Macleod, '*An Dotair Ban*', whose daughter was married to Rev. Norman Macleod of the Free Church in North Uist. Pole quickly discovered that one of the major difficulties on South Uist was that the factor had no authority to act in Cluny's absence. Pole was offering government supplies of meal at a low price, but even in the midst of such a desperate crisis the factor stated 'I could not on my instructions, take it upon myself to purchase food on Colonel Gordon's account.' Instead the factor and some local farmers put money together themselves to buy emergency supplies from Pole. The factor and the priest then worked together to distribute these supplies to those in need.[lii]

Another criticism made by Pole was that the various sources of employment for the people, including drainage works and fisheries, had been stopped by Cluny, which denied the people any means to earn a living. Cluny blamed his tenants, writing in December 1846 that 'in a variety of cases where work has been offered to robust young men they have refused, alleging that the proprietor of the soil is by law bound to feed them.'[liii]

However, the consistent opinion of factor, priests and others who spoke with Pole was that the people would be willing to work if they were given the opportunity. Captain Pole reported:

> It is the want of work which has produced this state of things. What an awful reflection it is, that at this moment the wealthy heritor of these islands is not employing the poor population; by doing which he can alone save them, and improve his own estate.

It was the prevailing belief of the time that, even in times of hardship, people should earn their living, and it was the responsibility of landlord and government to ensure that they could do so. John Chisholm, who was so moved by the plight of his people and who had assisted with the distribution of supplies, tried to address this issue. In Odo Blundell's *Catholic Highlands of Scotland* we read:

> Amongst the benefits conferred by Mr Chisholm was the branch road down to Lochboisdale, which he was the first to propose.

Poverty and Famine

This was at the time of the famine in 1846–1848. Mr Chisholm felt that the people were being supported by charity, and proposed making the road so as to give them employment, and the means of earning their food. At the meeting when this proposal was made, the factor, Dr Alexander McLeod, shook his fist in Mr Chisholm's face, but he later sent an apology, when the road had proved itself to be so great a boon. In reply to the angry factor, Mr Chisholm had merely whistled, a favourite practice of his.[liv]

From a 21st-century point of view this philosophy can be criticised, but similar schemes can be found across the Highlands. The so-called 'Committee Road' in North Uist was likewise built at the time of the famine, under direction of the Free Church Destitution Committee. Chisholm's concern for his people saw him make every effort to help them within the ideology of the day.

As the widespread destitution caused by the failure of the potato crop became known, an inquiry was held to discover whether the parochial boards, who were responsible for poor relief in each parish, were working adequately. As a result, in March 1847 Mr W A Peterkin arrived in South Uist, and met with various individuals including the factor, *An Dotair Ban*, and the priest, John Chisholm. He could not meet with the Established Church minister Roderick Maclean, for he had suffered 'a stroke of apoplexy' a couple of days earlier. Peterkin was startled and disapproving to discover that the factor was the only ordained Church of Scotland elder to sit on the board and that the two Roman Catholic priests were also members of the board. Clearly he did not understand the good ecumenical relations which existed for the benefit of the people on South Uist!

Peterkin raised the case of Widow Ann Gillies on South Uist, who was rumoured to have died of starvation and had received no visit from the Inspector of the Poor and no medical attendance other than a visit from the factor's wife. *An Dotair Ban* himself, however, gave his opinion 'as a medical man' that he had

Faith in a Crisis

frequently seen her in the past, she was asthmatic, and had died from natural causes.[lv]

The question of whether or not anyone actually died of starvation on South Uist and Barra was a controversial one. As we have seen, both the sheriff, Charles Shaw, and the priest, John Chisholm, alluded to rumours to that effect. The allegation that two people had died on Barra of starvation reached the defensive Cluny in February 1847. In immediately refuting these allegations, Cluny similarly drew on the testimony of his factor, *An Dotair Ban*, that he had known the individuals, they had been sickly for years, and had died of natural causes. Cluny described his factor as 'a medical man who, before he took the charge and management of my property in the Hebrides, was looked up to and consulted as the most experienced and best doctor in the district.'[lvi]

It was only the word of 'the most experienced and best doctor in the district' which stood between John Gordon of Cluny and the charge of allowing his tenants to die of starvation. That doctor was also his factor, a man under extreme pressure and without the means to prevent the crisis unfolding around him. The conflict of interest is unmistakeable.

Eviction and Emigration

The rage for emigration: leaving the islands

The ministers and priests of all denominations shared in short term measures to alleviate the poverty and suffering of the people, but longer term solutions were needed. By the later 1840s many people in the islands and beyond saw large scale emigration as the only viable way of dealing with the problem.

Emigration was a familiar concept in North and South Uist. In the later 18th century, many people left Uist for America in search of a better future. As the first settlers wrote home of their new lifestyle, more and more chose to follow. Writing in the 1790s, Rev. Allan MacQueen of North Uist described the situation:

> From 1771 to 1775, several thousands emigrated from the western Highlands to America, among whom were more than 200 from North Uist. These in turn gave their friends at home the same flattering accounts that induced themselves to go, so that these countries would in a short time have been drained of their inhabitants, had it not been for the American War. ... Since the close of the war, the rage for emigration has broken out again in different parts of the Highlands.[lvii]

Measures were taken for a time to limit emigration, as the landlords needed the population for the labour intensive kelp industry. Everything changed, however, as that industry collapsed and the landlords concentrated on enlarging their sheep farms to make the land profitable. The people's income decreased and their rent arrears began to build. From the 1820s onwards many were encouraged, persuaded and compelled to move from more fertile land to the less productive margins. Some continued to move

Faith in a Crisis

south to the mainland or to cross the Atlantic, sometimes with the financial help of the landlords. As poverty increased through the 1840s, the emigration of a large part of the population became seen more and more as the only solution to the poverty of the people.

A steady flow of migrants left North and South Uist, some eagerly seeking new opportunities, others perhaps reluctantly seeing little future at home and accepting the help on offer. But the poverty crisis which developed in the mid-1840s brought a new urgency to the situation. By 1849 Gordon of Cluny had shifted his position completely from denying that there was any problem to declaring that the crisis was so severe that emigration was the only solution:

> Your memorialist [Cluny] finds himself in possession of a property with a large population, the greater portion of which are, from no fault of his and from no cause attributable to him, utterly and entirely destitute, without employment, without motive or object for exertion, and without a sufficient quantity of land from which they can extract a subsistence, or the means of purchasing what the land fails to yield. … Such a population is a burden too great on the property, for the proprietor and for the country.[lviii]

In North Uist, Lord Macdonald had long since encouraged emigration. Charles Shaw explained 'There have periodically been extensive emigrations to the colonies within my recollection. All classes have gone. About the year 1840, many of the poorest left North Uist, Lord Macdonald having, from his own funds and from other sources, largely assisted them.'[lix]

But there was a problem. Many of the people did not want to leave, no matter how difficult their circumstances at home, and no matter what incentives were offered to them. The desperate years of the famine were followed by a new crisis. In both South Uist and North Uist, forced evictions took place which caught the nation's attention and have remained ever since as a deep scar on the history of the islands. And implicated along with landlords and factors, rightly or wrongly, were those ministers who lived alongside and cared for the people. What part did they really play in the clearances on Uist?

Notice to remove: clearance

Just as Gordon of Cluny's handling of the famine had brought him nationwide criticism, so his approach to emigration would also provoke outrage. By the late 1840s he had become convinced that the only way to make his island properties profitable was to get rid of a large section of the population. In this he was not alone, but the methods employed by his factors on his behalf were extreme.

Concern was initially raised over the condition of some families from South Uist and Barra who ended up in the cities of the south with no means of supporting themselves. In December 1850, the *Caledonian Mercury* reported on the arrival in Edinburgh of 23 destitute people from Barra:

> These poor creatures had been ejected from their holdings in the Island by the factors of Colonel Gordon of Cluny, the proprietor, and not knowing where to seek shelter, they had wandered to Edinburgh, where they understood their landlord was residing, in the hope that he as their natural protector would do something for their relief. They accordingly, cold and hungry as they were, presented themselves at his mansion in St Andrew Square, but found he was not at home.

Similar events occurred in Glasgow, where some of Cluny's tenants were stranded for a while en route to Canada. When they finally arrived in Canada, the Canadian authorities were horrified by their condition and by the lack of provision made for them on arrival. Dr Douglas, the medical superintendent at the quarantine station of Grosse Ile, stated 'I never, during my long experience at the station, saw a body of emigrants so destitute of clothing and bedding; many children of 9 and 10 years old had not a rag to cover them.' At a time when emigrants were flooding into Canada from famine-ravaged Ireland, this was quite a statement. The Canadian emigration agent, Mr Buchanan, was equally disapproving of Cluny and pointed out, 'To convey to this port emigrants possessing no resources whatsoever, and without a provision of some kind for their progress westward, is to subject them to great distress and certain discouragement.'[lx]

Although there was some sympathy in the British press for the poverty-stricken Highlanders, the decision of Cluny and other landowners to promote emigration was still widely seen as the only solution to the problem. It was at this point, however, that stories began to spread of the methods used by Cluny to compel the people to leave. By November 1851 there were allegations in the Canadian newspapers not only that Cluny had made false promises to the people but that some people had been physically forced on board the ships. The *Aberdeen Journal* repeated these claims with sceptisicm.

> The Quebec statement is in itself utterly improbable... Can it be believed that in the present day a policeman, a ground officer and two constables could frighten and chase a whole body of Highlanders to the mountains – that they afterwards caught twenty of them like wild beasts – and that by producing a pair of handcuffs the men were so terrified that they all agreed to go on board a ship for Canada![lxi]

Improbable or not, the rumours of clearance and forced emigration refused to go away. Donald Macleod's *Gloomy Memories*, published in 1856, contained alleged eyewitness accounts of the same events. And thirty years later, when the Napier Commission was gathering evidence in South Uist, the stories resurfaced. John MacKay, now a 75 year old crofter, remembered the notorious evictions:

> I saw a policeman chasing a man down the machair towards Askernish, with a view to catch him, in order to send him on board an emigrant ship lying in Loch Boisdale. I saw a man

who lay down on his face and nose on a little island, hiding himself from the policeman, and the policeman getting a dog to search for this missing man in order to get him on board the emigrant ship.[lxii]

Media attention had already been drawn to events on the neighbouring island of North Uist. Here there was an established pattern of emigration. Charles Shaw, sheriff-substitute, suggested to the Poor Law Enquiry of 1843 that the people were eager to accept Lord Macdonald's financial assistance to leave.

> When the people look to the difficulty of procuring subsistence at home, and receive good accounts from their friends in the colonies, their aversion to going abroad is diminished, and emigration on their part is altogether voluntary.

Later in his evidence, however, it becomes plain that 'altogether voluntary' is something of an exaggeration.

> The numbers offering to emigrate were increased by Lord Macdonald's giving notice of removal to those crofters, who were inhabiting less fertile parts of the parish, but who had not expressed their desire to emigrate or remove to other and better crofts on his property which were about to be left vacant by the emigration of the tenants or occupants. The notice to remove had the effect of deciding some to emigrate who were previously doubtful.[lxiii]

In spring 1849 such notices of removal were served on around one hundred families living in the Sollas area. By this time Macdonald's debt-ridden estate was under the control of trustees, and the chief agent acting on their behalf was Patrick Cooper, whose advances would soon be spurned by Jessie Macdonald. The families were offered free passage to Canada, but refused to leave. They continued to sow crops and work the land, and when Cooper and Shaw arrived to evict the people from their homes,

Eviction and Emigration

they were met with resistance and retreated. At the end of July a second attempted eviction took place, this time backed up by thirty constables armed with truncheons who had been brought from Inverness. Four men who had been involved in the original resistance were arrested. The evictions continued until most of the people agreed to sign a pledge to emigrate in the spring. The confrontation, the evictions and the trial which followed were widely reported in the newspapers. Many of the Sollas families moved to land at Locheport which was hopelessly infertile. After two years of hardship, trying to make a living out of unyielding ground, many of those who had originally come from Sollas boarded the *Hercules* for Australia in 1852. This ship, chartered by the Highland and Island Emigration society, would sail into its own troubles with an outbreak of smallpox taking place on board.

We will be left with the dregs: was denomination the cause?

In North Uist, those selected for emigration in the late 1840s were mainly associated with the Free Church. In South Uist, it tended to be Roman Catholics who were ejected from their homes. In both islands those who carried out the clearances were members of the Established Church. In a society where religious controversy was topical and where everyone was at least nominally associated with one branch of the church, many people believed they were being evicted from their homes because of their religious denomination.

This belief was particularly strong in North Uist, where Lord Macdonald and his factors were so vehemently opposed to the Free Church. Not only was the Free Church minister, Norman Macleod, evicted from his home and denied anywhere else to live, but the people's requests for a site for a place of worship were rejected and the meeting house they tried to build was torn down by the factor. Norman Macleod stated that some of his people were driven from their homes as a direct consequence of trying to build this meeting house and supporting the Free Church. He told the Select Committee on Sites for Churches (1847):

> Two of them are still without lands, living as cotters, and supported at present, I think, by destitution meal from Glasgow. One of those ejected got his lands back again last year, and three of them were obliged to emigrate to America; of those three two of them in particular were persons who gave us the use of their houses for worshipping in on Sabbath days and week days, and entertained our Free Church agents when they came that way.[lxiv]

In the same report, Norman Macleod made it clear that the Sollas district was at the heart of his Free Church ministry.

> We meet for worship in the district of Sollas, in the parish of Trumisgarry, not in the centre of the parish; it is there we meet

1. Lochmaddy Pier

2. The ruins of Sponish House (now rebuilt), home of the Shaws

3. The 'Committee Road'

4. Kilmuir Church, once the parish church of North Uist

*5. Finlay Macrae's now ruined farmhouse on Vallay,
seen from across the strand*

*6. The Established Church and manse at Trumisgarry, where
Norman Macleod ministered until the Disruption*

7. The Free Church and manse at Paible, which were only built once Lord Macdonald had sold his estate

8. Balranald House, North Uist

9. *The grave of Father James MacGregor*

10. *Interior of the Roman Catholic church at Iochdar*

11. *Interior of the Roman Catholic church at Ardkenneth*

12. *Church of Scotland at Howmore*

13. Interior of the church at Howmore, with its traditional central communion table

14. Roman Catholic church at Bornish

15. Interior of the church at Bornish

because the number of the inhabitants there is larger than in any other district.[lxv]

When Sollas was identified for clearance, the pro-Free Church *Inverness Advertiser* was quick to highlight the religious dimension:

> It is strange, passing strange, that this district of Solas is inhabited solely by adherents of the Free Church – in other words, the 600 or 700 beings ejected, with one or two exceptions, are Free Churchmen![lxvi]

Similar fears existed in South Uist, where a deliberate policy of introducing new tenants in place of local tacksmen saw Protestant incomers taking over lands from the South Uist Roman Catholics. Writing in 1917, Odo Blundell observed that the chapel at Bornish, built in a sizeable community, later stood alone, with no house within a mile of it,

> The Clanranalds, since they abandoned the Faith, were not personally hostile to their Catholic tenants, but their factors, and the underlings of these factors, have done a vast amount of evil by artfully and covertly supplanting or ejecting the poor, helpless Catholics, and by introducing and fostering in their places Protestants from North Uist, Skye and Harris; while the Catholics have been expatriated and compelled to remove to more friendly climes.[lxvii]

The close relationships which existed between landlords, factors and the Established Church ministers and elders added to the fear that denomination was the primary reason for eviction. In 1827 Duncan Shaw, factor to Clanranald (the landlord preceding Gordon of Cluny), had written a letter which highlighted the co-operation with the Established Church ministers,

> I beg… that in the event of any assistance [to emigrate] being granted, their heritors and their Factors, or these gentlemen joined with the established Clergy, be allowed to select the families to whom assistance is given.

However, Shaw went on to explain his reasons, and the heart of his selection policy was economic.

> If the Proprietors are not allowed to exercise very considerable influence in selecting the Emigrants, assistance will be given where it is not required, the most wealthy and industrious of our Population will Emigrate, and we will be left with the dregs. With regard to Clanranald's Estate, my object is to clear two particular Districts particularly well calculated for pasture, where the poorest of the People and worst of the Subtenants reside, and where the greater part of our inferior kelp is manufactured.[lxviii]

The Free Church and Roman Catholic members of the community were particularly vulnerable to eviction not primarily because of their religious denomination but because of their poverty. At the Disruption, the division had taken place broadly along socio-economic lines in the islands, with most of the poorer people turning their back on the Established Church of the landlords. The majority of those who had been hit hardest by the failure of the kelp industry and had the greatest rent arrears belonged to the Free and Roman Catholic churches. While their denomination may have been a factor – particularly, for example, in the case of those Free Church families who defied the landlord and tried to erect a meeting place – it was on the whole a desire to make the land more profitable which led the factors and landlords to instigate clearances. The earlier clearances in North Uist had taken place long before the Disruption. They evicted the poorest members of society – those whom Duncan Shaw called 'the dregs' – not primarily because of their religion but because of their poverty. The over-riding motivation was a desire to rid the land of a needy population, and the social make-up of the different churches meant that Free Church and Catholic families were the most affected, but not primarily as a result of their religious affiliation.

Religion is not averse to the duty:
Finlay Macrae and the Established Church

Among the letters of Bishop Andrew Scott, superior to the priests on Uist, is one from Dr Coll MacDonald of Lochshiel, dated 22 December 1839. MacDonald writes to the Bishop:

> I think it is a philanthropic Duty to send them to possess good land. I think Religion is not averse to the duty. Even if compulsion is necessary, which it will be.[lxix]

It was a question facing ministers and priests across northern Scotland, and not least in North and South Uist. As the landlords placed ever greater pressure on the people to leave, was it the role of religion to encourage emigration, or to oppose eviction?

On an official level, the churches were largely silent on the questions of emigration and eviction. Emigration was widely believed throughout society to be the only feasible answer to the Highland crisis, and many – although not all – ministers and priests held this view. An interesting example is Dr Norman Macleod, the leading Glasgow Church of Scotland minister who cared passionately about the Highlanders and was so active on their behalf at the time of the famine.

Dr Macleod saw at first hand the wretched condition of many who found themselves in Glasgow as a result of the profound changes affecting the Highlands and Islands,

> The Highlanders who come here are poor people, or children of poor people ejected from crofts. They ... are rouped out and, leaving their native place, are at length landed at the Broomielaw, where they are left without labour or work. The next time we hear of them is, that they are in the infirmary for some infectious complaint and they are sometimes here for a year or two in the lowest state of misery.

Dr Macleod was clear that evictions were leading to great suffering, but rather than blaming the landlords he blamed the government, for the tax changes which brought about the failure of the kelp industry. He stated that 'I am forced to the conclusion that it is to emigration alone we are to look for relief from the evils which have for such a long time past hurt that country', and he worked to promote schemes which offered genuine assistance to the settlers in their new country. Dr Macleod also believed that most ministers across the north of Scotland agreed with him.

> We corresponded with factors, subfactors, ministers, schoolmasters, and resident proprietors in the Highlands; and with the exception of one or two individual clergymen, the answer from the whole was precisely as you have stated – the combined efforts of emigration and education as the only two means to which they looked for relief.[lxx]

One of those who certainly believed in emigration was Finlay Macrae of Kilmuir church in North Uist. In 1837, Finlay wrote in the New Statistical Account, that 'it is necessary to find some proper outlet for the excess of population by emigration, and thus to increase the quantity of land possessed by each family.'[lxxi] In these views, as we have seen, he was far from alone. But Finlay's reputation has been damaged because he was so closely allied with those who were prepared to drive the people from their homes in order to seize their land. As recently as 1990, a book containing oral testimony from the people of North Uist stated, 'The Rev. Finlay Macrae is remembered for his treachery.'[lxxii]

Finlay was present throughout the Sollas disturbances, attempting along with Sheriff Shaw, Patrick Cooper and James Macdonald of Balranald to persuade the people to leave. The pro-Free Church *Inverness Advertiser* commented sarcastically on his involvement at the time.

> We have not the least wish to disparage the amount of sacrifice made by Mr Macrae in quitting his pastoral duties, and the care of his twelve mile square farm, which he finds leisure to conjoin with them, to attend upon the authorities.[lxxiii]

Throughout the Sollas disturbances the *Inverness Advertiser* was firmly on the side of the people, but a counter balance is provided by the *Inverness Courier*, which stated that 'The Rev. Macrae deserves the very highest credit for his conduct throughout this distressing affair.'[lxxiv]

Finlay believed wholeheartedly in emigration as part of the solution to the highland problem, but he was not one who blamed the islanders themselves for the difficulties they faced. Writing to the *Glasgow Herald* in 1851, he defended the character of the people, saying, 'The charge, so extensively and so injuriously circulated, and unfortunately believed, of want of industry in the inhabitants, is altogether without foundation... Their character is abused because they are not known.'[lxxv]

Finlay was both a friend of the authorities and a believer in emigration. He used his position to try to persuade the people to emigrate, but also offered practical assistance to those being evicted despite the fact that he was dealing with members of another congregation. He had an interview with Lord Macdonald, the intention of which apparently was to persuade the proprietor not to use violence. In addition, he put up bail money to allow the release of at least three of the four men taken prisoner during the riots, and was the only man willing to provide a 'heavy bond' as surety which would allow the people to remain in North Uist until next year, one of their principal objections to emigration being that it was now too late in the season. Despite making no compromise of his own belief that emigration was the best thing for the people, Macrae used his money and influence to attempt to make the situation as smooth for the tenants as possible, and in doing so offered more short term practical assistance than other members of the clergy.

Faith in a Crisis

Finlay's response was an individual one, and he did not represent all the other members of Uist Presbytery. The account of the evictions of South Uist and Barra people from Lochboisdale in Donald Macleod's *Gloomy Memories* contains great condemnation for the Established Church minister of Barra,

> The conduct of the Rev. H Beatson on that occasion is deserving of the censure of every feeling heart. This 'wolf in sheep's clothing' made himself very officious, as he always does, when he has an opportunity of oppressing the poor Barra men, and of gaining the favour of Colonel Gordon. In fact, he is the most vigilant and assiduous officer Colonel Gordon has. He may be seen in Castle Bay, the principal anchorage in Barra, whenever a sail is hoisted, directing his men, like a gamekeeper with his hounds, in case any of the doomed Barra men should escape.[lxxvi]

Beatson was a Greenock man who came to Barra in the summer of 1847, at the height of the poverty crisis. His character is hard to establish from Uist Presbytery minutes, owing to his repeated absence from meetings. However, when his co-operation in forcing Gordon of Cluny's tenants aboard overcrowded and insanitary boats bound for Canada is borne in mind, it is difficult to have much sympathy with his excuse for absence from these meetings, that 'he could not undertake the fatigue of a journey to Carinish'.[lxxvii]

The Christian duty of non-resistance:
Norman Macleod and the Free Church

In 1849, Norman Macleod of the Free Church saw the involvement of a large proportion of his congregation in a nationally publicised riot, the arrest, trial and imprisonment of four of their number, and their eventual eviction from their home firstly to infertile ground at Locheport and finally, two years later, overseas to Australia. The *Inverness Courier*, defender of Finlay Macrae, was critical of Norman's absence during these events, observing that he 'did not appear, either to counsel the people in the presence of the authorities, or to assist the latter by his presence.'

The *Inverness Advertiser*, in response to criticism, did attempt to offer an explanation. Although admitting they have received no communication from Mr Macleod on the matter, they insisted that,

> It is somewhat too much to expect that ... he was to countenance by his presence the perfecting of so gross an instance of legal oppression upon a portion of his own flock, and which must have revolted every feeling of his nature.[lxxviii]

Norman did not have the resources or influence available to Finlay to intervene in the crisis. His only practical intervention – the supply of character references for the men charged with rioting – inexplicably arrived too late to be of any use. But Norman saw his principal role as offering spiritual consolation and guidance to his people as they faced hardship. The *Advertiser* tells us,

> The poor people had another Sabbath in their homes, and were privileged, under very distressing and persecuted circumstances, to hear another impressive discourse from the Rev. Norman Macleod, from the words, 'They cried unto the Lord in their trouble, and He delivered them.' At the close, he gave them the soundest advice, which even those they deem their oppressors could not but commend.[lxxix]

Clearly, a sermon to which even the evictors could not object must have contained no violent sentiments, and this is revealed in the issue of 14 August, when the *Advertiser* stated that,

> We know, from positive information, that the Rev. gentleman was most indefatigable in inculcating upon the poor people the Christian duty of non-resistance to the constituted authorities, and had he not been so, there can be little question that they would have encountered more formidable opposition than women and children.

In advocating non-resistance, Norman Macleod joined churches of all denominations across Scotland. Finlay similarly was praised by the *Courier* for preaching non-resistance. It is this policy of urging the people to accept their miserable fate which has led to the greatest criticism of the clergy, who have been accused of betraying the people through a combination of greed, fear and self-interest.

Finlay Macrae's concern was not to prevent the evictions but to ease present discomforts in the firm belief that the people were moving on to a far better life overseas. Nevertheless, it was clearly in his material interests to support the policy of his patron and landowner, and he benefitted from the creation of larger farms. For these reasons he could be vulnerable to the accusation of acting at least partially out of self-interest. But Norman Macleod, minister to those who were suffering in North Uist, had very little to lose – yet he too urged the people to submit. The policy of non-resistance went far deeper than mere self-interest.

The Christian belief throughout society, in all denominations, was that resistance to the authorities was wrong, even when the people were faced with unjust hardship. In 1843, the Free Church offered similar advice to those being oppressed for breaking away from the Established Church.

> The General Assembly, while they earnestly exhort the people to a faithful and uncompromising adherence to their religious principles, would solemnly impress upon them the Christian duty of patient endurance, refraining from all acts of force or violence, which this Assembly must ever strongly condemn and deplore, and would unite with them in prayer to God to grant them a speedy and effectual delivery from their trials and afflictions.[lxxx]

Even in defence of their religious beliefs, the Free Church saw no justification for violence. Hardship was looked on as a trial to be endured and resistance to authority was wrong according to Scripture. This was not a new theology developed as a convenient response to the clearances, but a deeply held world view. These ministers advocated non-resistance not out of fear of the landlords but fear of God.

The newspaper reports of the Sollas evictions express sympathy with the plight of the people, but no support for rebellion. Even the *Inverness Advertiser*, so vocally opposed to the evictions, enters into debate with the *Inverness Courier* over which of the two ministers on North Uist deserves the most credit – and not censure – for the lack of violence which ensued. 'It is much to be lamented if any act of violence takes place on the part of the people,' states the *Advertiser*.[lxxxi] Resistance was frowned on by society at large, and the clergy, as a part of that society, believed it to be wrong.

Norman's primary concern was with the eternal salvation of his people, and thus he sought to support and guide them through the difficulties they faced. The best – heaven – was yet to come. Just as he urged them, when starving, not to steal flour, so he now urged them not to sin by violently resisting attempts to drive them from their homes. He had nothing to lose by standing up to Lord Macdonald, and he had shown both during and since the Disruption that he was not afraid to make his views known. He urged the people not to offer violent resistance both through concern for their spiritual condition and, perhaps, also through a more practical concern. Norman, himself evicted from his home, was aware of the weakness of the people in the face of the might the landlords could summon in protecting their Victorian land rights. In Sollas the threat of opposition brought over thirty constables armed with ash truncheons from Oban. The chance of rebellion on behalf of the people against the authority of the law and the vested interests of the landowning classes was slim; the clergy of all denominations would have known this and would therefore have been very unwilling to incite their people to rebellion which would inevitably lead to greater oppression.

Those who have criticised the ministers for advocating non-resistance have often pointed to the inordinate influence of these men over the people. JI Macpherson, writing in Alexander Mackenzie's *History of the Highland Clearances* in the 1880s, stated:

> They regarded the minister as the stern oracle of truth, and the strict interpreter of the meaning of the ways of God to man.'[lxxxii]

The implication has been that the ministers were held in such awe that their advice was responsible for persuading the people to submit. But this too should be questioned in North and South Uist. Finlay Macrae has been blamed for persuading the people to leave, but it is questionable that he held much influence over a Free Church community which had already rejected his ministry. An exchange during the riots which was reported in the *Inverness Advertiser* confirms the lack of respect for him among the Sollas crofters,

> The reverend parish minister before referred to was in a most excited state, from being placed in a new and uncalled for position – haranguing the people of another fold – and with the greatest emphasis articulated, 'It is a shame for a woman' to speak in meetings such as the one he was in. This was met by a derisive

laugh and by the question, 'Does not a woman reign over us all?' and one very slyly asked the divine 'Are you and we all not born of women?'[lxxxiii]

There is no doubt that Norman Macleod held a greater influence over his people, but in Sollas many of the people were prepared to ignore the pleadings of their pastor and fight for their homes. Rebellion did take place, with people on both North and South Uist reluctant simply to accept the will of the landlords, in spite of the protestations of their ministers.

They are much attached to the soil:
John Chisholm and the clergy of the south

In June 1843, South Uist priest John Chisholm gave evidence to the Poor Law enquiry. He was quite clear that the landlord's policy of moving people to create new sheep farms was to blame for the widespread poverty.

> He attributes the deterioration of the situation of the crofters to a number of small farms being thrown into large ones, and the former holders of them being thrown a burden on the community; and hence, the poor press more upon those living on their own means than formerly.

Chisholm stressed the provision of employment, rather than emigration, as the most effective solution for the island's problems. He knew that, whatever their poverty, his people had no desire to leave.

> He cannot say that any of the people in the island are inclined to emigrate – they are much attached to the soil.[lxxxiv]

Gordon of Cluny had purchased his South Uist and Barra estates in 1838, and as we have seen Chisholm's superior Bishop Scott had urged him to ensure good relations with the new landlord.

> Were the Catholics to submit implicitly and apparently with cheerfulness to all his plans and to all his orders whatever they may be, and to speak always favourably of him, and if the protestants were to thwart him in anything, the whole island would soon become entirely Catholic. For some years it will require very great prudence on the part of the Catholic Clergymen and on the part of the poor catholics, and if you will always act according to what I have said, you will find it will ultimately be for your own interest and for the interest of Religion in these Islands.[lxxxv]

Eviction and Emigration

Bishop Scott clearly had no idea, when he wrote his no doubt well-meaning advice, of the terrible events which were to unfold, and there is no evidence that John Chisholm took his instructions to heart in the context of eviction and emigration.

Chisholm was critical as we see above of the clearance of people to make way for larger farms, and was deeply troubled by their poverty. His attempts to provide relief brought him into open conflict with the factor, *An Dotair Ban*. There is also some evidence that Chisholm was involved in opposing the worst excesses of the Lochboisdale removals. In the description of the Lochboisdale clearances in *Gloomy Memories*, there is a reference to an unnamed priest who was probably John Chisholm, although he could possibly have been either Donald MacDonald (Barra) or James MacGregor (Iochdar),

> One stout Highlander, named Angus Johnston, resisted with such pith that they had to handcuff him before he could be mastered; but in consequence of the priest's interference his manacles were removed, and he was marched between four officers on board the emigrant vessel.[lxxxvi]

This story was repeated with a little embellishment by John MacKay in his evidence to the Napier Commission thirty years later,

> A man named Angus Johnston … was seized and tied upon the pier of Loch Boisdale; and it was by means of giving him a kick that he was put into the boat and knocked down. The old priest interfered, and said, ' What are you doing to this man? Let him alone. It is against the law.'[lxxxvii]

Like Finlay Macrae, this priest intervened to make the short term situation for the tenants easier, but he was surely powerless to prevent the actual eviction. He had not the resources or influence of Finlay, but the evidence suggests that he was prepared to stand up to the factor and even the landlord to offer what help he could to his people.

A Fresh Perspective

A different system of management:
Thomas McLauchlan and a challenge to emigration

As Uist was battered by the failure of the kelp industry, the loss of the potato crop and the horror of evictions, the priests and ministers responded with limited efforts to relieve the suffering of the people. Finlay Macrae, as a believer in emigration, encouraged the people to leave but offered some practical assistance. Norman Macleod sought to give spiritual guidance and consolation to the people through their hardship, and to set their eyes on a heavenly goal, and John Chisholm appears to have intervened where he could on behalf of his people. By contrast, Henry Beatson of Barra was said to have actively assisted the authorities to force the people to leave. Each of them, although with a different slant, responded from within the ideology of the day – emigration was regarded as an inevitable consequence of an unsustainable situation, and resistance was wrong. None of them offered a clear voice speaking out against the events which were taking place on Uist. That voice came from elsewhere.

Thomas McLauchlan was minister of St Columba's Free Church in Edinburgh, and would later become a noted writer and Moderator of the Free Church. In 1850, aged 35, he published a pamphlet, *Recent Highland Ejections Considered*, which presented a very different point of view to that which was repeated time and again in the newspapers. McLauchlan took the example of the clearances from Sollas, and sought to demonstrate firstly that they were unjust and unnecessary, and secondly, that the whole country should be greatly concerned by them.

Thomas travelled to North and South Uist to see the islands for himself. He explained:

> The cry of over-population, destitution, the necessity of emigration, and so forth, was ringing in my ears, and I was not a little wishful to know whether there was any, and what ground for it.

But Thomas presented a very different picture of the islands for his readers.

> The common idea, we believe, is that these islands are bare, barren and cheerless – really unfit for human habitation, and that transportation to the colonies is a privilege, not an infliction, to the people ... A visit to the Uists, however, is sufficient to remove [preconceived opinions] at once. North and South Uist are fine, fertile islands, presenting features unusually attractive, whether to the searcher after the useful or the picturesque.

Thomas McLauchlan went on to praise the land in the Sollas district particularly – 'whatever Lord MacDonald's commissioner may say to the contrary' – and to argue that vast clearances had worsened the overcrowding among those who were left, and had left vast tracts of potentially fertile land in the hands of a few 'speculators', rather than using them for the benefit of the people. He pulled no punches, likening the forced emigrations to 'white-slave traffic' and describing the infertile eastern fringes to which some had been removed as 'Botany Bay'.

McLauchlan then appealed to the consciences of his readers, and used one argument after another to urge them into action. In contrast to the caricatures of idle Highlanders often bandied around, he stressed the quality of those now leaving the country. He pointed to the number of servants, teachers, ministers and soldiers who came from these Highland communities. He emphasised their spiritual worth – 'Many of these are men of God, the preserving salt of our land,' – and questioned the impact

A Fresh Perspective

on Scotland should all these worthy people be lost to other lands. He pointed to the financial burden of Highland displacement on the cities, and warned country dwellers that the clearances would soon come to the Lowlands. He urged the Free Church in the south to support its northern followers, and finally he warned of ultimate judgement,

> The cause of Christ in the Highlands has suffered not a little from the ejectment system; and whatever men have done or may do now, we doubt not that there is a record on high which will one day speak with a voice that will strike terror into the hearts of the men that were engaged in it.

This was a very different message and rhetoric to that of Norman Macleod. McLauchlan called for public meetings and a parliamentary inquiry. His solution was not depopulation but a new and more just approach to the management of the land. 'I venture to say,' he wrote, 'that quadruple the population might be supported by the Uists under a different system of management, and that with certain advantage to the proprietor.'[lxxxviii]

No-one else with influence on Uist was saying that yet, but thirty years on the picture had changed. The Napier Commission was set up in 1883 in response to continued agitation by crofters, and considered many of the issues which McLauchlan had highlighted thirty years earlier. The commissioners came to North and South Uist to gather evidence in May 1883. They heard from crofters, factors, clergymen and teachers. Their evidence reveals both that the memories of the dreadful events of the 1840s and 50s were still very vivid, and that general attitudes towards emigration had changed.

The priest at Iochdar, Donald McColl, gave a statement on behalf of the crofters which looked back to the forced evictions.

> We are in no way inclined to emigrate, while there are plenty lands in the country for us, for the next hundred years. ... We

Faith in a Crisis

> desire not to see revived the cruel and forced evictions, as carried out in 1819 and 1851, when many were bound hand and feet, and packed off like cattle on board the vessel to America. The recollections of ill-treatment and cruel evictions towards many in those days operates unfavourably on the minds of the present generation towards emigration.[lxxxix]

The Church of Scotland minister in South Uist was the same Roderick Macdonald who had succeeded his father-in-law Roderick Maclean when that man finally died in 1854. In 1883, after a long ministry and a lifetime on the islands, he was described in the evidence of one Roman Catholic witness as 'a good friend to the country.' Roderick himself praised the character of the people, and gave his opinion that policies of removal in the past had been carried too far.

> To emigration one feels many objections; it deprives the land of its best inhabitants – we lose the bone and sinew of the country; and considering the violent wrench required to enable a Highlander to tear himself from his native rocks, one has not the heart to advise them to leave.[xc]

Norman Macleod had died two years earlier, in 1881. The Free Church minister at Carinish, North Uist, gave evidence to the Commission. He was questioned about people being targeted for eviction because they belonged to the Free Church. He admitted he had heard of that in the past, but that nowadays landlord, tenant and church were 'on the best of terms in that respect.'[xci]

The Church of Scotland minister in North Uist at the time of the Napier Commission was John Alexander Macrae, son of Finlay. He gave a detailed account of the evictions from Sollas and the later emigration to Australia from Locheport. Describing himself as 'a very bad farmer', he stated that he was in favour of increasing the land held by the people.

A Fresh Perspective

The commissioners asked him why, when his father had given a very favourable account of the condition of the people in the New Statistical Account in 1837, such widespread evictions had taken place so soon afterwards. Finlay's son replied, 'I can hardly account for that except in the way of clearing the land for others.'[xcii]

Thomas McLauchlan would have agreed.

Conclusion

The ministers and priests of North and South Uist in the mid-19th century were confronted by events which brought great suffering to their people. As spiritual leaders, the clergymen of Highland communities have often been portrayed as at best passive and at worst complicit in the hardship of the people. When the islands were ravaged by famine, the clergy of all three denominations worked to alleviate the immediate suffering around them. The three individuals we have examined in detail – Finlay Macrae, Norman Macleod, and John Chisholm – lived in starkly different circumstances and viewed the world from different perspectives. For example Norman, who urged his starving people not to steal shipwrecked flour, was the only one to clearly state that the famine was sent by God to turn the people from sin. But despite their differing perspectives, all three men were involved in raising awareness of the problem, distributing relief and encouraging schemes which offered employment. Their national churches also worked from their different resources to help the people.

The widespread opinion through much of Scottish society was that the islands were over populated, and that emigration was necessary. Very few voices spoke out with an alternative viewpoint. In Uist, a longstanding pattern of emigration was followed at this time by two notorious cases of forced eviction.

Suspicion existed among the people that their religious denomination was the cause of their removal, but the evidence suggests that the driving factors behind the evictions were primarily economic.

Finlay Macrae was a firm believer in emigration and tried to persuade the people to leave, but he also used his means and his influence to alleviate the short-term difficulties they faced. Norman Macleod's emphasis was on offering spiritual consolation. Both ministers advocated non-resistance, which has since been controversial. However this was not an approach dreamed up in response to the clearances and in deference to the landlords, but was a deeply held world view which had already been applied in other situations, including the defence of religious freedom. It is also unlikely that that the clergymen, at least of the Established Church, were held in such reverence that their advice held significant weight with the people. The Roman Catholic priests were prepared to stand up to the landlords and oppose emigration, but had little influence to do more than bring comfort and short term assistance to the people.

There is very little to suggest that any of these men was motivated primarily by self-interest, and all three sought to offer some help from within their existing ideologies. However, none of the clergymen on Uist saw it as his role to speak out clearly against the events taking place. It took voices from outside, like Thomas McLauchlan, to present a different point of view which challenged the very concept of emigration as the best solution to the islands' problems. This was radical at the time but had become more widespread by the time of the Napier Commission, and would eventually bring about genuine change.

Notes

i. Allan MacQueen, 'North Uist', *Statistical Account of Scotland*, vol. 13, 1791–99
ii. Clanranald Papers, Letter from Duncan Shaw, 25 March 1827, GD201/4/97
iii. Proceedings of the Scottish Parliament, 27 September 2000
iv. Angus Macdonald, *North Uist – a sketch of its history*, vol. 2, p55
v. ibid.
vi. Testament of Rev Finlay Macrae, SC29/44/10
vii. Finlay Macrae, 'North Uist', *New Statistical Account*, vol. 14, 1837
viii. Macdonald, *North Uist*, vol. 2, p67
ix. Napier Commission, 1884, p812
x. *Aberdeen Journal*, 21 August 1850
xi. Kilmuir Parish Church Parish Records, 31 March 1850, CH2/113/00
xii. St Cuthbert's Parish Records, 22 April 1850, CH2/685/02
xiii. Quoted in Ewen MacRury, *A Hebridean Parish*, 1950
xiv. William Ewing (ed), *Annals of the Free Church*, 1914
xv. Third Report from the Select Committee on Sites for Churches (Scotland), 1847, p19, p23
xvi. MacRury, *A Hebridean Parish*, p32–3
xvii. Presbytery of Uist Minutes, 29 September 1829, CH2/361
xviii. Fourth Report of the Commissioners of Religious Instruction, Scotland, 1837–8, p165
xix. Presbytery Minutes, 27 March 1839

Notes

xx. Macdonald, *North Uist*, vol. 2, p53
xxi. Third Report from the Select Committee on Sites for Churches (Scotland), 1847, p21–2
xxii. Third Report from the Select Committee on Sites for Churches (Scotland), 1847, p23–4
xxiii. Third Report from the Select Committee on Sites for Churches (Scotland), 1847, p25
xxiv. Presbytery Minutes, 29 November 1843
xxv. Angus Macdonald, *South Uist*, vol. 1, p114–6
xxvi. Oban Letters, 14 August 1840, OL/1/32/3
xxvii. Odo Blundell, *The Catholic Highlands of Scotland*, 1917, p45
xxviii. *Caledonian Mercury*, 29 May 1848
xxix. Fasti Ecclesiae Scoticanae; Napier Commission, 1884, p706; MacDonald, *South Uist*, vol. 1, p86
xxx. Oban Letters, 4 March 1835, OL/1/10/15
xxxi. Presbytery Minutes, 24 November 1841; Oban Letters, 26 November 1841, OL/1/37/8
xxxii. Oban Letters, 14 May 1832, OL/1/7/12
xxxiii. Fourth Report of the Commissioners of Religious Instruction, Scotland, 1837–8, p157
xxxiv. Poor Law Inquiry (Scotland), Appendix I, 1844, p337
xxxv. Poor Law Inquiry (Scotland), Appendix II, 1844, p363
xxxvi. Correspondence from July 1846 to February 1847 relating to the measures adopted for the relief of the distress in Scotland, p189
xxxvii. Correspondence from July 1846 to February 1847 relating to the measures adopted for the relief of the distress in Scotland, p190–1, 259–61, 300
xxxviii. Macdonald, *North Uist*, vol. 2, p16
xxxix. Principal Acts of the General Assembly of the Church of Scotland 1847–50, p44

Notes

xl. Acts of the General Assembly of the Free Church of Scotland 1853–7, p143

xli. Principal Acts of the General Assembly of the Church of Scotland 1847–50, p44

xlii. TM Devine, *The Great Highland Famine*, 1988

xliii. Correspondence from July 1846 to February 1847 relating to the measures adopted for the relief of the distress in Scotland, p260

xliv. Third Report from the Select Committee on Sites for Churches (Scotland), 1847, p21

xlv. Poor Law Inquiry (Scotland), Appendix I, 1844, p650

xlvi. Macdonald, *North Uist*, vol. 2, p17

xlvii. *Glasgow Herald*, 11 August 1851

xlviii. Presbytery Minutes, 29 November 1848

xlix. Correspondence from July 1846 to February 1847 relating to the measures adopted for the relief of the distress in Scotland, p195

l. *Inverness Courier*, January 1847

li. Third Report from the Select Committee on Sites for Churches (Scotland), 1847, p27

lii. Correspondence from July 1846 to February 1847 relating to the measures adopted for the relief of the distress in Scotland, p293–9

liii. Correspondence, p265

liv. Odo Blundell, *The Catholic Highlands of Scotland*, 1917, p49–50

lv. Second annual report of the Board of Supervision for the Relief of the Poor in Scotland, 1847, p62–64

lvi. Correspondence, p350

lvii. Allan MacQueen, 'North Uist', *Statistical Account of Scotland*, vol. 13, 1791–99

lviii. *Aberdeen Journal*, 12 September 1849

Notes

lix. Report to the Board of Supervision by Sir John McNeill, 1851, p118

lx. Papers relative to emigration to the Northern American colonies, 1852, p9, p17

lxi. *Aberdeen Journal*, 19 November 1851

lxii. Napier Commission, 1884, p707

lxiii. Poor Law Inquiry (Scotland), Appendix II, 1844, p367

lxiv. Third Report from the Select Committee on Sites for Churches (Scotland), 1847, p24

lxv. Third Report from the Select Committee on Sites for Churches (Scotland), 1847, p19

lxvi. *Inverness Advertiser*, 24 July 1849

lxvii. Odo Blundell, *The Catholic Highlands of Scotland*, 1917, p45

lxviii. Clanranald Papers, Letter from Duncan Shaw, 25 March 1827, GD201/4/97

lxix. Oban Letters, 22 December 1839, OL/1/29/15

lxx. Poor Law Inquiry (Scotland), Appendix I, 1844, p642, 648, 651

lxxi. Finlay Macrae, 'North Uist', *New Statistical Account*, vol. 14, 1837

lxxii. David Craig, *On the Crofters' Trail*, 1990, p57

lxxiii. *Inverness Advertiser*, 7 August 1849

lxxiv. *Inverness Courier*, August 1849

lxxv. *Glasgow Herald*, 28 July 1851

lxxvi. Donald Macleod, *Gloomy Memories*, 1857

lxxvii. Presbytery Minutes, 10 September 1851

lxxviii. *Inverness Advertiser*, 7 August 1849

lxxix. *Inverness Advertiser*, 31 July 1849

lxxx. Acts of the Free Church, 1843–7, p19

lxxxi. *Inverness Advertiser*, 31 July 1849

lxxxii. Alexander Mackenzie, *A History of the Highland Clearances*, 1883

Notes

lxxxiii. *Inverness Advertiser*, 31 July 1849
lxxxiv. Poor Law Inquiry (Scotland), Appendix II, 1844, p366
lxxxv. Oban Letters, 14 August 1840, OL/1/32/3
lxxxvi. Donald Macleod, *Gloomy Memories*, 1857
lxxxvii. Napier Commission, 1884, p707
lxxxviii. Thomas McLauchlan, *Recent Highland Ejections Considered*, 1850
lxxxix. Napier Commission, 1884, p779
xc. Napier Commission, 1884, p729
xci. Napier Commission, 1884, p809
xcii. Napier Commission, 1884, p809–816

Bibliography

Church sources

Acts of the General Assembly of the Free Church of Scotland
Free Church of Scotland Assembly Proceedings, 1851
The Principal Acts of the General Assembly of the Church of Scotland
Minutes of the Synod of Glenelg
Minutes of the Presbytery of Uist
Minutes of the Kirk Session of Kilmuir Parish Church, North Uist
Fasti Ecclesiae Scoticanae
Oban Letters – Western District (Scottish Catholic Archives)

Parliamentary sources (by date order)

Fourth Report of the Commissioners of Religious Instruction, Scotland, 1837–8
First report of the Select Committee on Emigration, 1841
Poor Law Inquiry (Scotland), Appendix I & II, 1844
Correspondence from July 1846 to February 1847 relating to the measures adopted for the relief of the distress in Scotland
Second annual report of the Board of Supervision for the Relief of the Poor in Scotland, 1847
Second Report from the Select Committee on Sites for Churches, 1847
Third Report from the Select Committee on Sites for Churches (Scotland), 1847

Report to the Board of Supervision by Sir John McNeill, 1851
Papers relative to emigration to the Northern American colonies, 1852
Report of Her Majesty's Commissioner of Inquiry into the condition of the Crofters and Cottars in the Highlands and Islands of Scotland, 1884 (also known as the Napier Commission)

Other sources

Clanranald Estate Papers – Letters from Duncan Shaw
Testament of Rev Finlay Macrae, SC29/44/10
The Statistical Account of Scotland vol. 13
The New Statistical Account of Scotland vol. 14

Aberdeen Journal
Caledonian Mercury
Glasgow Herald
Inverness Advertiser
Inverness Courier

Thomas Brown, *Annals of the Disruption*, 1893
Odo Blundell, *The Catholic Highlands of Scotland*, 1917
Ray Burnett, *Benbecula*, 1986
Henry Cockburn, *Circuit Journeys*
David Craig, *On the Crofters' Trail*, 1990
TM Devine, *The Great Highland Famine*, 1988
William Ewing (ed), *Annals of the Free Church*, 1914
James Hunter, *The Making of the Crofting Community*, 1976
Bill Lawson, *North Uist in History and Legend*, 2004
Allan MacColl, *Land, Faith and the Crofting Community*, 2006
Angus Macdonald, *North Uist – a sketch of its history* (unpublished)
Angus Macdonald, *South Uist – a sketch of its history* (unpublished)
Alexander Mackenzie, *A History of the Highland Clearances*, 1883

Bibliography

Thomas McLauchlan, *Recent Highland Ejections Considered*, 1850
Donald Macleod, *Gloomy Memories*, 1857
Ewen MacRury, *A Hebridean Parish*, 1950
David Paton, *The Clergy and the Clearances*, 2006
John Prebble, *The Highland Clearances*, 1963
Eric Richards, *Storm over the Highlands: debating the Highland clearances*, 2007
Eric Richards, *The Highland Clearances: people, landlords and rural turmoil*, 2008